Great Minds Think Alike

10 STEPS TO UNLOCKING SUCCESS IN YOUR LIFE

Ritchard G. Fewell
Certified Fitness Trainer
National Academy of Sports Medicine
Functional Movement Specialist

DISCOVER HOW TO PUSH THROUGH ANY BOUNDARY AND NEVER SETTLE FOR MEDIOCRITY AGAIN

Copyright © 2015 Ritchard G. Fewell. All rights reserved. No portion of this book may be reproduced mechanically, electronically, or by any other means, including photocopying, without written permission of the publisher. It is illegal to copy this book, post it to a website, or distribute it by any other means without permission from the publisher.

Ritchard G. Fewell
rgf38@msn.com
Stamford, Conn.
www.ReactFitness.com

Limits of Liability and Disclaimer of Warranty

The author and publisher shall not be liable for your misuse of this material. This book is strictly for informational and educational purposes.

Warning – Disclaimer

The purpose of this book is to educate and entertain. The author and/or publisher do not guarantee that anyone following these techniques, suggestions, tips, ideas, or strategies will become successful. The author and/or publisher shall have neither liability nor responsibility to anyone with respect to any loss or damage caused, or alleged to be caused, directly or indirectly by the information contained in this book.

ISBN: 978-0-692-69430-5

SUCCESS AWAITS YOU!

Get my FREE Top 10 Health Tips for Your Personal and Fitness Success!

Have you ever felt like your position in life could be better or your mental and physical state be improved upon? This may help you.

Here's what a few coaching clients are saying about Ritchard:

"After completing a year long intensive chemotherapy protocol, I went to Ritch and asked him to 'bring me back to life.' I had known some clients of his at the time that experienced amazing results with their workout regimen. What I didn't know was the impact he would have on my overall outlook on life. Ritch is the TOTAL PACKAGE. His training programs are very challenging but a lot of fun. His comprehensive knowledge of wellness and nutrition is second to none."

"But it's the positive attitude he brings to every aspect of his life daily that is truly inspiring. He taught me so much about my body, myself and my soul."

~ Jennifer Harris

Pick up your FREE Health Tips!
www.ReactFitness.com

Dedication

Through my life I have had people who have impacted me greatly and have helped make me who I am today. I'd like to dedicate this book to them.

To my father Richard Fewell. You always provided for us and taught us valuable life lessons. I get my knack for writing from you.

To my mother Geraldine Fewell. May you rest in peace. You were the neighborhood mom and all the kids loved you. You took care of the household and took great care of us. I miss you.

To my sister Renee Davis my brother-in-law Malcolm Davis my beautiful nieces Courtney and Alexis Davis and all my relatives. Family is everything.

To my circle of good friends. Ray Boyd, Norberto Barroso, Lamar Pringle, Maurice Ludicone, and Sam Gohar.

To the Marchants. Genuinely great people!

To my extended family of amazing fitness coaching clients. You enable me to do what I love. You are all positive, great souls and in super shape. I appreciate all of you.

To Donna Kozik. The best writing coach in the business. I knew I found my inner author and would be able to complete my writings when I found you.

Great Minds Think Alike

About Ritchard Fewell

Ritchard G. Fewell is a NASM (National Academy Of Sports Medicine) Certified Personal Trainer, Lifestyle Coach and FMS (Functional Movement Screen) Specialist.

He has been featured in *Family Circle* magazine and The Fitfluential Fitness and Nutrition Blog for his weight loss transformation.

He is a member of The IDEA World Fitness Organization and has attended numerous Mastermind and Fitness Business Summits.

His philosophy and approach to success in your life be it personal or professional begins with having the right mindset. He believes that everyone can attain a higher order of life by working towards their purpose once it is found.

Ritchard has overcome his own hardships as a youth growing up in the inner-city and struggling to find direction and a purpose.

An unconditioned mind, body and a warning from his doctor to start living healthier or face a shortened life led him to the gym where he gained confidence, mind power and a new physical appearance.

Conquering his weight loss struggles, Ritchard was able to lose 90 pounds and realize his passion for physical fitness. It was this intervention where he found his destiny and the passion to help others achieve their goals and change their lives as well.

Ritchard currently resides in Stamford, Connecticut and his Personal Training Business, REACT Fitness, is based in Greenwich where he coaches his clients.

He always says "you know you love your job when you look forward to Mondays."

In his spare time Ritchard enjoys working out, writing, watching sports, hanging with friends, family and his Shihtzu Tessa.

Contents

Chapter 1: Having Vision 3

Chapter 2: Setting Goals 13

Chapter 3: Are You Willing? 23

Chapter 4: Overcoming Perfectionism 33

Chapter 5: Discover & Learning 43

Chapter 6: Relationships 51

Chapter 7: Connection 59

Chapter 8: Overcoming Procrastination 65

Chapter 9: Developing Confidence 73

Chapter 10: Having Perseverance 79

NOTES 83

VISION

"If you fail to create your own vision you will live your life through someone else's eyes."

~ Ritchard G. Fewell

Chapter 1: Having Vision

"If you want to build a ship, don't herd people together to collect wood and don't assign those tasks and work, but rather teach them to long for the endless immensity of the sea."

~ Antoine de Saint-Exupery

One of the first elements of success is having vision. Vision is seeing what's not there...yet. It is the ability to project your thoughts and goals

forward while having the end result in mind. It's putting energy, attention and focus on where you want to go. After that, you want to be able to share it with others so they will follow you where you lead. For instance, Fitness or Life Coaches get their coaching clients to buy into their system by creating a vision for their clients. Getting them to visualize how much joy and satisfaction it would bring to achieve their goals.
Projecting is the first step and you must do that without self-doubt.

Self-doubt comes when a person is unsure or afraid of saying where they want to go. It's like sitting in your car at the end of the driveway...and sitting...and sitting...and sitting. Sometimes making a decision seems like a lot of pressure. What if I make a mistake? What if I choose the wrong vision? What if pursing that vision is a waste of time? Or what if you reach it and are disappointed because it's not all that it's cracked up to be? You will never know until you get there right? But you do know that the place where you are is not where you should be forever.

It reminds me of a quote attributed to Michelangelo: "The greatest danger for most of us is not that our aim is too high and we miss it, but that it is too low and we reach it."

There's another quote from Robert Frizt that says, "If you limit your choices only to what seems possible or reasonable, you disconnect yourself from what you truly want, and all that is left is a compromise." How many times do you feel frustrated because you follow what you think would be the best choice for others (and not yourself) or because it was the "expected" thing to do? You end up following the pack instead of leading it. You end up sacrificing your own dreams for someone else's. Without having a clear vision of what you want, you'll always find yourself lost, confused and aimless.

Another problem is when you want to go everywhere--all at once. You take a left out of the driveway then turn back and go right. And then turn back and go straight. Or you travel a bit and forget where you are going and become lost, meandering up and down streets that seem to have made sense at the time, but you're never quite sure and question everything. You've forgotten your original destination and, more importantly, your original vision.

Many times the solution is perceived to be to "work harder." Action is definitely part of achieving vision for sure but driving faster in the wrong direction is not the way to achieve anything.

So how does someone look to develop a clear vision about what they want? The first thing you want to do is spend some quality time with yourself. Instead of latching onto the first "sounds good" that comes to mind, ask yourself, what do you really want out of life? Where do you want to go? Some people are able to picture their vision best when spending quiet time with themselves at the beach or while taking a walk in nature. Others use the energy of busy streets and lots of people to tap into a deeper calling within them—they feel it in the middle of hustle bustle. Others like to write their thoughts down in a journal or online note-taking application, ruminate on them a bit and then create a vision statement for themselves.

Leaders of a Faith such as Priests or Reverends amass hundreds and hundreds of followers to attend their service. Their powerful influence and vision calls on Parishioners to develop a system of belief. They possess the strength to lead and relay their message of what life should be and that vision is always kept in mind until what they see for themselves comes to fruition. They are consistently rejecting the actions and decisions that don't match the bigger picture. Their passion for a higher power is what drives their vision.

Once you find your passion you will find your

purpose. Once you find your purpose you can start to create the vision of your journey.

GOALS

"Our goals can only be reached through a vehicle of a plan, in which we must fervently believe, and upon which we must vigorously act. There is no other route to success."

~ Pablo Picasso

Chapter 2: Setting Goals

"It's better to be at the bottom of the ladder you want to climb than at the top of the one you don't."

~ Stephen Kellogg

No book about success would be complete without a chapter on goal setting. Whether it's a Fitness goal, a Professional or a personal goal, this gives you an opportunity to really assess what you've declared about what you want in life.

Are you satisfied with where you are at in your financial affairs, health, relationships and career?

If not, time to take a look at your goals. What have you set as your benchmarks for success in each of those areas? How would you feel if you achieve those successes?

J.C. Penney was a man who didn't mince words. (He also appreciated a great deal.) Once he said, "Give me a stock clerk with a goal and I'll give you a man who will make history. Give me a man with no goals and I'll give you a stock clerk." You want to set goals so you have purpose and direction in your actions. And, not to stress you out, if you don't have goals you may find yourself waking up one night staring blankly at the ceiling realizing you've lived an aimless life and a life that will become filled with regret. It is better to fail over and over again then not to try at all. You goals will manifest with planning and work. You have to believe that you have a purpose and to not stop until you find that purpose. Don't die before you are dead.

You have to make up your mind and start setting a goal--one that stretches you without breaking you--gives you something to aim for and something to work for. And, when you do that, you will never lose. This one step of selecting a goal and working to achieve it gives you personal power and intent. It gives you a life worth living and a feeling of joy, happiness and a change in a new and positive direction.

The late, great Jim Rohn said "You cannot change your destination overnight, but you can Change your direction overnight." Actually, with all respect to Mr. Rohn, it doesn't even take that long to change direction. It simply takes a split second to make a decision. The main thing is to make that decision to go from what you don't want, to what you do. It takes a commitment to that decision and a relentless will to achieve a higher life.

A common goal-setting technique involves the acronym SMART--perhaps you've heard of setting SMART goals. Smart stands for:

- Specific
- Measurable
- Attainable
- Realistic
- Timely

First, you want your goal to be specific. A specific

goal sets you up for success and gives you the ability to accomplish it. It also means you'll recognize it when you achieve the goal. Think like a reporter when you're setting a specific goal, asking yourself who, what, where, when, why and, instead of how, which. (Meaning which requirements and constraints can you identify?)

Second, it should be measurable. What numbers can you assign to your goal to measure your progress and attainment? This will help you stay on track and give you reason to celebrate when you accomplish the goal.

Next is to verify your goal is attainable. You want to not only identify the steps you'll take to acheive your goal, but the time frame involved. At the same time, realize you'll grow along the way, adopting an attitude of confidence and great capacity as you meet your mini-goals along the way.

Then comes "realistic," as you want your goal to represent an objective that's not only attainable, but also you're willing to work towards it. At the same time, don't make it easy but something that will represent progress and growth on a number of levels, say personally and professonally.

Finally, there's "timely." You don't want to meander towards your goal, but instead create a sense of urgency. You have to basically become a predator by making that goal a top priority and something that you want badly. It has to get done and you won't stop until you achieve it. A lion doesn't need to be told when to hunt. They just hunt instinctually.

Having a nebulous date sometime in the future will not cut it. Instead you want to anchor your goal within a specific timeframe otherwise you may never achieve what you set out to do. You want to make sure it is achieveable. Ask yourself what else needs to happen--both in and out of your control--to make the goal happen. If it's realistic and has happened before, it can happen again.

Just a note—the T in SMART can also stand for tangible. A goal is tangible when you can experience it with one of your five senses. Some say that you have a better chance of making it happen if you think tangible, because it will become more "real" and your journey will be more evident.

WILLINGNESS

"Willingness opens the doors to knowledge, direction and achievement. Be willing to know, be willing to do, be willing to create a positive result. Be willing, especially, to follow your dream."

~ Peter McWilliams

Chapter 3: Are You Willing?

"We must be willing to get rid of the life we've planned so as to have the life that is waiting for us."

~ Joseph Campbell

Willingness, it seems like an innocuous word, but when you start to ask how willing you are to grow, to change, to forgive, well, it takes on many other connotations.

To not be willing is to be in resistance. How can you tell when you're in resistance? It can show up in a number of ways. Knowing what you "should" do, but don't. (Although the word "should" has a lot of resisting ideas of its own.) It could be a nagging feeling of taking some action that could lead to your greater good, yet, for whatever reason, you don't take that action. Resistance can also be more subtle. Days, weeks, months go by and you realize you've slowly been sinking in a certain area: relationships are always on edge, financial matters ebb into the red, health declines until the things that used to be great are now only good or fair to middling. You start to become a victim of the duldrums of life. You start to develop a defeatus attitude and begin to fall into self-oppression.

There was a story in *The Daily Guru* that says deserts are dry because of a form of resistance. The email newsletter reported that rain actually falls high above the desert, but fails to reach the ground below because the water evaporates when striking a zone of hot and dry air, otherwise known as resistance. Humans have created their own zone of hot and dry air that vaporizes ideas, growth and truths. If you look to overcome this zone of resistance by being willing, you will find good things raining down.

So what does it look like to be willing? It's an ease, calmness and a relaxing into a better way. It's dropping the "shoulds" and the "can'ts" and the "what ifs" and instead taking a moment and being with "what is." You can even do that right now by stopping your mind, your thoughts and taking a breath. If you really want to see how this works, take a moment and repeat out loud, "I am willing." Keep reinforcing the positive. That's when you come to the realization that you want more out of life.

In her book *Fearless Living*, Rhonda Britton puts it simply by saying "Being willing makes you able." When you drop the resistance and the stories, you'll find yourself lighter and more willing--more able--to allow. More able to relax and receive. Feel how nice that is?

Related to allowance is everyone's favorite concept: patience. It's actually much easier to embrace patience when you get in the practice of dropping resistance, stories, fears and more to become more willing. You become more driven by knowing that the work and time that you put in will not go unrewarded.

Why would you want to go through all this? You

would for a couple of reasons. First, you desire to evolve to a higher level of life. Someone reading these words wants to stay the same. You want to continue to grow as a person and experience all life has to offer. It's a good reason to drop the resistance and become more willing. Also, how would you like things to become easier in life? It can happen--if you are willing. Willing to accept change and move forward. Willing to put aside your fears and attain what you want from life.

"One can never consent to creep when one feels an impulse to soar," said Helen Keller. If you've felt the impulse to be better and do more in life, relax and drop the effort and instead become more willing.

Moving into Action

There comes a point when the resistance is dropped the willingness is there. So what's next? It's time to move into action. The difference between the one's who succeed and the ones who don't is action.

The problem most people have is that they get back into their heads and start the litney of "need to's" as in "I need to do this and I need to do that and I need to do this, this and this." Although taking action is desired, we don't want you to get back in your head a place of analysis and paralysis. Instead, start with small steps, even baby steps, while remaining alert and aware of what comes next.

The late Robert Schuller said, "Better to do

something imperfectly than to do nothing flawlessly." It's time to move forward and show others--and yourself--what you can do.

Perfectionism

" Push yourself to achieve excellence and don't confuse that with perfection, for if you think that you are perfect, you will stop learning and when you stop learning, you stop living and striving for excellence."

~ Ritchard G. Fewell

Chapter 4: Overcoming Perfectionism

"But I am learning that perfection isn't what matters. In fact, it's the very thing that can destroy you if you let it."

~ Emily Giffin

Many people throw around the idea of being a "perfectionist" with a great deal of pride. Although it may impress at a job interview, living life as a perfectionist can be a nightmare. The idea of never being satisfied with "good enough" means condemning yourself to always striving for better, better, better and not enjoying the blessings life has right now.

The flip side is to become so obsessed and worried with having things "perfect" (and, really, who is the one creating the end-all definition of perfection?) that you never even begin the journey. It becomes an excuse for never getting started.

Dr. David Burns puts it this way, "Aim for success, not perfection. Never give up your right to be wrong, because then you will lose the ability to learn new things and move forward with your life. Remember that fear always lurks behind perfectionism. Confronting your fears and allowing yourself the right to be human can, paradoxically, make yourself a happier and more productive person."

There's a lot to be said for mistakes. They are valuable in that they demonstrate to you what not to do. Mistakes are lessons in learning. They teach us better ways to solve problems. Most of us have heard how many times Thomas Edison tried to invent what we now call the light bulb and failed miserably time after time. In fact, when it finally continued to burn, he just expected it to fail and waited for it to go out. He waited and waited. Can you imagine the feeling of exhilaration that started to grow when he realized that it wasn't going to go out? That he had done it? It must have been amazing but it would never have been felt (and I'd be typing this in the dark) if he didn't stick with it. One success makes one hundred failures worth it.

If you suffer from perfectionism, here are some

general ideas to keep in mind to overcome a tendancy that could be keeping you from success.

1. Take it easy on yourself. No one succeeds when they have a drill sergeant screaming in their ear. all the time. It's also not a matter of one giant leap from idea to success, but rather a series of steps along the way. Practice that and enjoy the journey. Also, be willing to release your idea of what has to be perfect. There's a big difference in importance between giving a presentation in front of your boss and making sure your books are all aligned on the shelf "just so."

2. Take it easy on others. Forcing your ideas of what's "perfect" on others is a sure road to tense relationships and extreme stress, for starters. People don't like to feel controlled (at best) or manipulated (at worst) or bullied (at very worst).

And they definitely don't like their perceived weaknesses called out. Consider things from others' perspectives and do unto others as you would like do unto you.

3. See the funny side of life. The tension felt by a strong sense of perfectionism means there's little room for seeing the humor in life. And, when you look around and relax your standards, you'll see a lot of opportunity to laugh, which feels good. It will also help you out when things don't go exactly according to plan. Let's think of someone who smiles and laughs through life and look for ways to hang out with them more often. You'll be happy you did. Joy is an emotion that we should all aim to experience. However, it gets hindered by constant worrying and trying to have everything in your life perfect. Sometimes due to

the pressure that you put on yourself by comparing your life to others that may be ahead of you or trying to meet their expectations. They must accept you for who you are or you don't need them in your circle and you must expect yourself to become greater and excel upward.

Because making mistakes isn't a mortal sin (in fact, the word "sin" simply means "miss the mark" in archery terms), don't use your fear of making them as an excuse to not get started in the first place. As Mary Morrissey tells it, a child who tumbles after trying out his first steps doesn't stay on the floor forever thinking, "That's it. I guess I wasn't meant to walk." Instead they get up and try again.

Those that don't stop are that ones who achieve. Those who forfeit their power and quest for freedom are the ones who are left wondering what the world looks like through successful eyes.

Discovery & Learning

"One of the key to learning is to have mentors who will help guide you for if you want to learn, you have to align with people who are smarter than yourself."

~ Ritchard G. Fewell

Chapter 5: Discover & Learning

"Live as if you were to die tomorrow. Learn as if you were to live forever."

~ Mahatma Gandhi

A Chinese proverb says that learning is a treasure that will follow its owner everywhere.

It's true, learn once and you will have something that no one will be able to take away from you.

It's been shown that learning keeps us "young at mind," and when you stop learning you start to grow old and stagnant.

At the same time, people have found that choosing what they learn can be an important part of the reasoning process. You can fill your mind with knowledge of the mundane or choose to go after the more esoteric--something that will challenge you to think and dream bigger.

And then there is the fun of thinking of things in the shower. Here's a list compiled by the site reddit of "random shower thoughts."

1. The object of golf is to play the least amount of golf.

2. Do Geese see God spelled backwards is Do Geese see God.

3. Instead of all the prequel and sequel movies coming out, they should start making "equels" - films shot in the same time period as the original film, but from an entirely different perspective.

4. I wonder how many strangers photos I'm in the backround of.

5. April Fools Day is the one day of the year that people critically evaluate news articles before accepting them as true.

6. Websites should post their password requirements on their login pages so I can remember what I needed to do to my normal password to make it work on their site.

7. Now that cellphones are becoming more and more waterproof, pretty soon it will be okay to push people into pools again.

8. Last night my friend asked to use a USB port to charge his cigarette, but I was using it to charge my book. The future is stupid.

9. "Go to bed, you'll feel better in the morning" is the human version of "Did you turn it off and turn it back on again?"

10. Your shadow is a confirmation that light has traveled nearly 93 million miles unobstructed, only to be deprived of reaching the ground in the final few feet thanks to you.

Learning and discovery continue long after high

school. In fact, high school can be the place where we learn how to learn.

One of the best ways to learn is by doing. How many times have you heard a toddler say, "Let me do it!" It's the adults who keep that child-like sense of wanting to try and do things who are likely to savor more out of life. Aristotle said, "For the things we have to learn before we can do them, we learn by doing them."

Think about how you can put into practice, a greater learning in life. One way to start is embracing the concept of curiosity. Keep it sharp and you will never become too advanced in age to appreciate what life has to offer. Another way to learn is to teach. It reinforces concepts in the one doing the teaching and shares the knowledge with others.

Remember that you are a compilation of the people you hang around with, too. Take a look at who is surrounding you and what you are learning from them. Nine people of positivity will breed a tenth. Ten people of negativity will breed an eleventh. Surround yourself with people who support your goals and dreams. This will enable your growth and growth will bring you closer to happiness.

You must never stop learning and striving for the right way to do things. You must seek to become wise because becoming wise will help you savor the marrow of life and enjoy all it has to offer.

Great Minds Think Alike

Relationships

"No road is too long with good company."

~ Turkish Proverb

Chapter 6: Relationships

"Relationships--of all kinds--are like sand held in your hand. Held loosely, with an open hand, the sand remains where it is. The minute you close your hand and squeeze tightly to hold on, the sand trickles through your fingers. You may hold onto some of it, but most will be spilled.

"A relationship is like that. Held loosely, with respect and freedom for the other person, it is likely to remain intact. But hold too tightly, too possessively, and the relationship slips away and is lost."

~ Kaleel Jamison

The Earth would be a lonely place without sharing it with someone else. Relationships take all on forms, shapes and sizes. Sometimes people meet before they can walk and know they will be life-long friends. Other relationships are briefer than brief, perhaps an exchange of smiles in an elevator or in line at the grocery store.

They all have something to offer, if you pay attention to the possibility.

For those longer relationships, there can be moments of pure joy and others of sheer frustration. How can you overcome those trying times? William James put it this way, "Whenever you're in conflict with someone, there is one factor that can make the difference between damaging your relationship and deepening it. That factor is attitude."

Have you ever had those moments when you're in the middle of the same old argument and you have an ah-ha moment. One that may prompt you to turn things around by saying, "You know, your right. I'm wrong. Let's work together on this." It can be one of the greatest feeling of relief and happiness--those times when we're willing to let go of being right and instead being willing to be happy or at least harmonious.

Many relationship issues are centered in expectations. What's assumed the other person will do or say. This is a formula for disaster and, when you think about it, lunacy. I've talked about the stress of trying to be a perfect you. Just imagine putting that stress on another person and "scripting" their lives for them. Donald Miller said, "When you stop expecting people to be perfect, you can like them for who they are."

One technique for improving relationships is practicing the adage of "walking a mile in their moccasins." How would you feel about things if you were in their shoes for a month, a week, a day and an hour? This not only applies to people close to us who we believe should "know better," but to those who we are jealous or envious of. You can admire what they have or what they've achieved, but would you really want to be them? Well, probably not. That's because you were put on this earth to be you. You are an individual a unique creation of God there is only one you.

Some people, especially business owners, lose

their way when they start thinking of people as part of a "target market" or "leads" or "prospects." What they are really talking about are people. And the best way to connect with people is to build relationships with them. You have to listen more than talk and give more than receive. It makes sense when you think about it, but many times it's easy to fall into the trap of what the "experts" recommend in holding back until the people pay. That's definitely trying to grasp the sand. People will come to you and believe in you if you are genuine and truly care. If they feel that you really want to help and have their best interest in mind. You need to make your message powerful. A Personal Trainer won't have many clients if people don't believe in his message and they feel that he/she truly doesn't have their interests in mind. You have to build relationships and create a personal and professional circle of great people.

Then there's the relationship you have with yourself. It serves as the foundation of all relationships. Do you treat yourself as your best friend or someone who shouldn't be trusted? Do you hold back in loving the one person who is with you 24-7 or do you fawn over the glorious human you are--the one with all your so-called faults and habits? Above it quotes Donald Miller reminding you to stop expecting people to be perfect. The same applies to the way you think about yourself. It's time to turn loving attention on the one who matters most.

Connection

"All things are connected like the blood that unites us. We do not weave the web of life; we are merely a strand in it. Whatever we do to the web, we do to ourselves."

~ Chief Seattle

Chapter 7: Connection

"Since you cannot do well to all, you are to pay special attention to those who, by the accidents of time, or place, or circumstances, are brought into closer connection with you."

~ Augustine of Hippo

Connection means realizing that you are not alone in anything. Not only is there a connection to other people, you are connected to animals, plants and even the air you breathe.

Alan Watts said it best: "I'll tell you what hermits realize. If you go off into a far, far forest and get very quiet, you'll come to understand that you're connected with everything." You will feel harmony.

This is important to realize because it means no one is alone in this world. Plus there is something bigger at work that what the mind can perceive. It's part of the past, the future and the present. It can be daunting or exhilarating--it depends on how you choose to look at it.

The energy of the connection is like a current running through everything. And you can pick up and feel the current or disconnect yourself from it--the choice is yours. When you do feel the lifeforce, however, you'll find not only an easier time here on planet Earth, but a feeling of exhilaration knowing you can tap into this universal energy anytime you wish. It's always a part of you--always has been and always will be. Lord Tennyson put it poetically, "I am a part of all that I have met."

The feeling of cause and effect becomes stronger the more you practice it. The first step is to be aware and notice who, what, when and where that goes on your life every day. When you think of the supposed "accidental" connections, you'll see that each is a minor miracle. A second step is to notice the impact you have on other people and animals. Would that dog from the shelter still exist if you didn't rescue it? How about the warning you shouted out to a small child getting ready to run in front of a speeding car? Although all events might not seem that impactful, you never know what a small decision and connection can mean to someone else.

Practice noticing a greater connection to life today and be aware of life's universal magic. Be the great person that God placed you on this Earth to be and with your power and positive presense you can lift people up.

PROCRASTINATION

"Only put off until tomorrow what you are willing to die having left undone."
~ Pablo Picasso

Chapter 8: Overcoming Procrastination

"Don't wait. The time will never be just right."

~ Napoleon Hill

Procrastination, or the art of putting off until tomorrow (or next week or next year) what can be done today, is a frequent block to success. Interestingly, it's usually the people who are doers in general who say they struggle with procrastination. There may be just one or two areas where it seems that they can't get things going.

In decades past procrastinators might have chosen

a crossword or walk in the woods instead of doing a task that becomes more and more pressing with time. These days there are all types of electronic devices and offerings to distract from doing what needs to be done. There can also be a false sense of "busy and productive" developed when actually we are busy doing nothing.

It reminds me of a quote from Henry David Thoreau: "It's not enough to be busy. The question is: What are you busy about?"

The good news is that we are all given the same amount of time in a day to "do." Money can't buy more time and science can't invent it. Time, like manna, cannot be hoarded.

There are four different reasons for

procrastination:

* A failure of motivation -- you're not feeling the drive to get started, move the project or idea along or finish it.

* A matter of organization -- things are in disarray and you're not even sure what the next step is to get going.

* A feeling of overwhelm -- this is a type of clutter of the mind where there's so much to think about that you don't know where to start.

* A feeling of paralysis -- this can be a combination of overwhelm, organization and motivation that add up to feeling stuck and unable to do anything.

Here are some ways to get over each of these:

To get moving, make up your own reward system. Make it something that will really motivate you to get the work started and completed. You can also try the "anti-good-feeling" method and recognize the unpleasant consequences of not completing the task. Accountability is always a good motivator, so consider getting yourself a buddy to check up on you. Finally, after you get the task done, also take note of that feeling of satisfaction!

To get organized, focus on one thing at a time. Many people aren't disorganized, they are just thrown by looking at all in front of them. But when you focus on one thing at a time, it gives you a place to put your concentration to the exclusion of other things. Also, instead of doing a major overhaul of life and planning tasks, start small with a daily to-do list and a calendar that's up to date.

To get out of overwhelming yourself, think about "chunking" and breaking the project up into tasks that are more do-able. Creating a step-by-step plan showing you these steps in order (and giving you something to check off) can also be helpful. Also, go for the "quick win" and the tasks that really don't take that long to do--it will help motivate you to keep going and stay out of overwhelm.

If you are feeling paralyzed at the thought of getting started, question your reasoning. What is the thinking behind doing the task in the first place? Is it necessary or something you think you "should" do? If it's necessary, what are you afraid or worried about? Talk the process out loud to see if your reasoning is sound, or bounce the problem off a trusted friend for his or her advice.

Confidence

"If you hear a voice within you say 'you cannot paint,' then by all means paint, and that voice will be silenced."

~ Vincent Van Gogh

Chapter 9: Developing Confidence

"Low self-confidence isn't a life sentence. Self-confidence can be learned, practiced, and mastered--just like any other skill. Once you master it, everything in your life will change for the better."

~ Barrie Davenport

Confidence, or how you present yourself, is vital in nearly every aspect of life. Unfortunately, many people struggle to find it, which can lead to perpetual low self-esteem and a vicious cycle of unsuccess. Characteristics of not being confident include nervousness, fumbling and being "sorry" when no apology is necessary. This can lead to anxiety, depression and loneliness.

Confidence is having an unshakable belief in yourself--one that may have developed after overcoming a fear. Everyone needs confidence to grow in body, mind and spirit. If you didn't develop some confidence along the way you'll find yourself stagnant and dissatisfied with life. Women, especially, can fall prey to low-self confidence and the lack of success it brings. What does self-confidence look like? Someone who is self-confident holds their head up high, speaks with assuredness and isn't afraid to say "I don't know" in answer to a question. (The last point being the opposite of what many see as self-confidence!)

People who are full of self confidence inspire it in

others--their audiences, friends, family and clients. Gaining confidence of others leads to success for the self-confident person.

Here are some suggestions for increasing your own self-confidence:

1. Begin now. Many people wait until conditions are "right" and then believe they'll take action and stop feeling fear. It doesn't work that way. Start with an activity that will banish the fear--even a small one will start to build your confidence.

2. Build your proof. One way you can develop more confidence is by reflecting on your past successes. Write down your wins over fear and build your record of proof.

3. Prepare for the best. Many times the greatest things we have feared come to pass. Instead of preparing for disaster, prepare for success. It's much easier to go down a road we already know in mind.

PERSEVERANCE

"Never confuse a single defeat with a final defeat."
                                      ~ F. Scott Fitzgerald

Chapter 10: Having Perseverance

"A winner is just a loser who tried one more time."

~ George M. Moore Jr.

Perseverance is about continuing on when you feel like quitting. It's a key to success for many heroes and also "regular people" who make their way through the day the best they can celebrating their successes and during the times of trial think "I'll try again tomorrow."

Developing a sense of perseverance is important

with any endevour, especially those that seem out of reach and take more time to accomplish. The stretching to achieve comes from the trying and the doing.

So, how do you develop more perseverance? It's more than "just keep going." It's about finding the tools and the thinking that will help you dig deep when you just want to quit. More than that, you can develop perseverance so you not only meet your goals, but learn to enjoy the process along the way.

One thing that makes quitting "not an option," is knowing what it is you want in life. It might be a specific goal such as scuba diving in Hawaii, losing weight or getting a promotion. Or it could be more general such as being a more peaceful person or better spouse. When you identify what you want in life, it's easier to become more determined to achieve it. In connection to this, know your values. What principles do you live by? What is non-negotiable to you? Keeping your values top of mind makes it easier to decide on the actions and activities that will support you in your goals.

Another aspect of perseverance is believing in yourself. Yes, it's great to get the support of others, but if you don't have the self-confidence in your own ability you're not likely to succeed. To strengthen your self-belief, think about the things in life you have achieved your goals. You can call on that muscle memory to go after your goals now.

That said, you do what to surround yourself with positive people--those who also have an optimistic outlook on life and goals of their own. You'll pick up on their energy and that will increase your own. More importantly, stay away from negative people who can zap your energy and your confidence. It's too easy to stay in the "why even try" mojo instead of going full speed ahead in pursuit of what you want in life.

Make your dreams so big that people who don't dream of becoming anything at all think you are crazy. It's ok to be afraid, but it's not ok to stay in a state of stagnation.

God has given you the great gift of life. Live it to the fullest and be your best you!

NOTES

NOTES

NOTES

NOTES

NOTES

NOTES

NOTES

Great Minds Think Alike!

"Ritch Fewell has been my Personal Trainer/ Coach for seven years. Through his teaching, I have learned to maintain a healthy weight while gaining mental clarity. He always says that laughter makes the toughest workouts easier and boosts you mood and achieving your goals will bring you joy and self worth. Ritch has given me the tools I need to continue on my journey to a healthy, happy lifestyle."

~ Sue Davidson

Ritchard Fewell is a National Academy of Sports Medicine (NASM) Certified Fitness Trainer and a Functional Movement Specialist (FMS). He has inspired hundreds of people to get fit physically and mentally and realize their purpose in life. He has been featured in *Family Circle* magazine and currently runs a mobile personal training business.

www.ingramcontent.com/pod-product-compliance
Lightning Source LLC
Chambersburg PA
CBHW031942070426
42450CB00005BA/468